TRADING SET
TRADING RULES

TRADING SETUPS WITH SUPPORT AND RESISTANCE

* ★ *

ONLINE TRADING
DAY TRADING RULES

MALINA PRONTO

Trading Setups: Trading Rules

Trading Setups With Support And Resistance:

Online Trading - Day Trading Rules

Introduction

One of the keys to being a successful day trader is to possess an inventory of rules that you simply consistently follow. Unlike a daily job where you'd have a boss looking over your shoulder, as each day trader, you will be your own boss and thus be liable for your own results.

By writing down and following your day trading rules, you'll create a system that reinforces your trading discipline and prevents you from making costly errors. during this article, I'm getting to share my three most vital day trading rules.

Rule #1: Manage Risk On Every Trade

This rule is basically the inspiration for my trading philosophy. It means on every trade I make, my first consideration isn't what proportion potential profit I could make, but what proportion money I could potentially lose. Too many traders focus an excessive amount of on the potential profit and overlook the importance of risk management. Before I make any trade, I do know what my downside is and therefore the price at which I will be able to exit the trade if it goes against me (my stop-loss). This ensures that no single losing trade is going to be catastrophic. As a trader, my goal is to hit consistent singles and doubles and not necessarily home runs.

Rule #2: Limit Midday Trading

Another key to becoming a consistently profitable day trader is to know the importance of the time of day. In terms of trading opportunities, not all times are created equal. Generally, there's far more volatility and volume within the stock exchange at the open and shut of trading and a pronounced lull in trading activity during the center of the day. Because day traders need volatility to form money and also must overcome their transaction costs, trading within the middle of the day is usually a nasty idea. To enforce this rule, I keep my eye on the clock and drastically reduce my position sizes and risk within the middle of the day (generally from 10:00 am -2:00 pm CST).

Rule #3: Review Every Trade I Make

I view every trade I make as a learning experience, both to find out more about the strategies and techniques I'm using also to gain information about the present market. one among the beauties of trading is that you simply get instant feedback on your decisions. During this review process, I focus my attention not on the results of the trade but on the choices I made. Was my position sizing ideal? Should I even have moved my stop-loss? Did I follow my risk management plan? As any experienced trader will tell you, there are repeatedly where poor trades find yourself being profitable while excellent trades don't compute. so as to enhance as a trader, it is vital that you simply learn from every single trade you place.

Conclusion

By following these day trading rules, I do know that I am often consistently profitable and make excellent risk/reward trades. While risk management may sound like an abstract principle, I implement it by knowing my stop-loss before placing any trade. I'm also conscious of the foremost opportune times to trade and limit my trading when conditions aren't ideal. Finally, I gain insight from every trade I make by having a radical review process. Take the time to write down down your trading rules to bring clarity to your trading and make sure you stay disciplined.

More E-Mini Trading Setups With Support and Resistance

It's not unusual to ascertain traders using support and resistance to line up potential trades. the foremost common trade I see among novice investors may be found out that envisions the worth action "bouncing" off an existing support or resistance lines. There are many versions of this particular trade, and it's commonplace to ascertain small investors implement this trade over and over. To make certain, using support and resistance lines as potential setups is extremely common.

Unlike the trade I described above, where the tiny traders are trying to find a bounce off a support or resistance line, I'm trying to find a continuation through a support/resistance line. This is sensible at several levels. First and foremost, I'm a trend-oriented trader and dislike trading against the trend. By definition, any bounce off a support or resistance line would entail a move against an existing trend, which are some things I avoid, especially during a strong trend. Secondly, so as for the worth action to maneuver through a support or resistance line it takes a medium, at the smallest amount, and typically a robust push to pierce the road. Inevitably, this strong push creates excess momentum which is carried through for 10 or 15 additional ticks, and people additional ticks are the prize I'm seeking to capture. This found out usually leads to a really violent and short trade because the momentum pushes the worth upward or downward at a high rate of speed. it's an exciting trade to observe and even more exciting to initiate.

When setting this particular trade up, I generally search for a robust support/resistance line which will intersect a longtime line . As an aside, I tend to like better to take this trade to the short side because the market tends to maneuver faster when heading downward. this will be attributed to panic selling, or long traders bailing out of short positions because the price action moves against them. In any event, I position my entry three or four points below the support/resistance line and await the worth to return to me. Needless to mention, it's never an honest idea to chase the worth action and it's rare on behalf of me to initiate an order. I would like to enter a trade at some extent of my very own choosing where I feel I even have the simplest chance of profiting.

Once you become familiar with spotting the found out, you will find it occurs two to 3 times daily. The trade is comparatively reliable if it occurs during a trending market, and therefore the trend doesn't necessarily need to be a robust one. On the opposite hand, I might avoid taking this trade when the market is during a well-defined channel. Breakouts or breakdowns out of channel formations are generally unreliable and typically fail. False breakouts from a channel formation look very enticing from the onset, but after moving three or four ticks in your favor they have a tendency to retreat back to the channel. Once within the channel, it's anyone's guess where the worth action may go as movement inside the channel is random, at best.

In summary, we've checked out a trade using support/resistance lines. rather than trying to find a bounce off these lines, we've outlined a straight that entails a continuation of a trend through known support/resistance.

we've noted that this trade is reliable when utilized in conjunction with a trending market, further we've cautioned against taking a straight out of very well-established channel.

How to Look for a Company That Sets Up Computer Systems for Traders

Now that day traders are starting to understand that not all computers are created for stock trading, they're turning to niche companies for assistance. If you are looking to shop for a computer for trading, then you'll first get to find a corporation that focuses on multi-monitor trading setups for day traders.

Focus on Buying Trading Computers vs. Gaming Computers

There are some day traders out there immediately who are using gaming computers, security systems, and other sorts of computers not specifically designed for day trading. a number of these systems are known to be fast and maybe upgraded extensively, but simply put, these aren't built for day trading professionals. Gaming computers are made for visual effects and running games seamlessly. this might sound great to a beginner in trading, but this is not enough. Trading computers are quite just graphics and speed. You're also getting to need multiple monitor connections to ascertain all of your running tasks. Ultimately, you would like each day trading computer that's made for traders, by traders; one that caters to your every need, which incorporates speed, space, cooling, and multiple screens.

Why Air and Liquid Cooling is vital

Running your computer for extended periods of your time, using multiple monitors, could cause it to overheat. this is often why it is vital to possess a computer for trading that's ready to handle extreme usage while remaining cool. this is often where liquid and air cooling systems inherit play. you will need to seek out a trading PC that comes with one or the opposite. If you select air, confirm that the system comes with a minimum of two fans. the corporate you purchase from should have a trading computer that comes with a sufficient cooling system, in order that your computer and data stay safe.

Properly Configuring Your Day Trading Computer

Your multi-monitor trading setup should be built with the components in mind. Not all components are compatible with each other and only a knowledgeable company is going to be ready to build you a PC that's harmonious for day trading. Many of the computers you will find on store shelves accompany inferiority components that albeit you upgrade, likely won't be ready to handle the tasks you would like to perform. In most cases, you will find a low-end processor with sufficient RAM and a standard disk drive.

In a trading computer, you are going to wish a top-quality processor, many RAM, and a minimum of one terabyte of disk drive space (solid-state hard drive). Another area that must be compatible is your multiple monitors.

It's recommended that each one of your monitors be of an equivalent make and model.

Buying your trading computer from a corporation that focuses on this area will make sure that you're getting a PC that comes with everything you would like .

The Importance of Day Trading Rules

"Trading Rules" may be a term that gets thrown around so often it's become cliché. At the beginning of my trading career, I got so uninterested in hearing about the importance of trading rules. Trying to make trading rules as a replacement trader is like trying to select a university major with zero work experience. How on earth can this be done?

First, let's address what your trading rules should cover. the foremost important purpose of trading rules is to attenuate your losses. for instance, what percentage times have you ever entered an edge, gotten stopped out, then watched price move within the direction of your original trade? this is often probably the only most frustrating part about trading and could be the rationale most traders fail. it is easy to acknowledge a trend and it seems crazy to understand with absolute certainty which way your market is moving and at an equivalent time, haven't any way of trading it because you lack trading rules to enter the trade with minimal drawdown (losses).

Your trading rules should incorporate an answer to the present problem. as an example, oftentimes I exploit a moving average or a pivot point on a chart and make rules that I will be able to belong above this level or flat (out of the trade) below this level. I even have named this strategy the toll booth strategy because I demand to be paid a toll if the market wishes to advance past my level. If it doesn't advance or if the market reverses before browsing my level, I even have lost a chance for a brief trade but I even have not lost any money.

The second thing your trading rules should cover is how far you'll let the trade run before taking profits. during this example, I'm getting to address the instrument you're trading as "your market." Statistically speaking, you ought to be conversant in how far your market usually goes in each wave before backing and filling (retracing). This measure is extremely important for brief-term trading. Using the ES E-mini as an example, I even have found this market will only move about 3 points during a single market wave that shows on a five-minute chart before retracing some portion of these 3 points.

The last item a trader wants is to realize two and a half points and need to give one and a half back to the market during a routine retracement. thereupon in mind, you'll be wanting to make trading rules that have a profit target of but 3 points per trade. Perhaps you discover that two points work well for you. So you'll be wanting to make trading rules that say you'll exit all or most of your position once you are up a minimum of two points.

Lastly, you would possibly consider incorporating a rule that addresses your position size. briefly term trading, there's no such thing as an honest trade or a nasty trade. you ought to trade an equivalent position size for each trade in order that your outcomes yield an equivalent wins and losses. When creating this rule, you ought to consider your account size first and foremost. The position size you trade should be in positive correlation with what proportion you've got in your account.

As you'll see, these are simple but powerful solutions to keeping you consistently profitable. If you've always considered Trading for a Living but lacked the proper set of Trading Rules [http://www.insidethetrade.net/], follow the link during this sentence to find out more about my trading rules or call me at the amount below.

Day Trading Rules to Live By

Most people looking to form money within the markets believe that the solution lies find some simple technical analysis strategies which will catapult them to profitability.

The truth is that trading isn't as simple as beginners believe. it's a profession, and like all profession, it requires a learning curve. Reading a book or getting a couple of simple "tips" isn't getting to turn you into a knowledgeable trader.

After studying for a length of your time, it isn't uncommon for college kids to start their look for the "holy grail."

They look for more indicators, chart patterns, gurus, alert services, or the newest secret day trading strategies and other things that will provide their answer to becoming successful.

But here's the very fact. Success lies within you .. and it won't come easy.

In fact, one of my favorite success principles is this:

"Successful people do what unsuccessful people are unwilling to try to to ."

Let's apply this to trading within the sort of my list of "Day Trading Rules to measure

By" ... all of which need to do more with you than with the market.

The consistency you would like it in your mind, not within the market. Many within the market get frustrated because the market often behaves differently than they expect. you cannot believe the market to be consistent. it's largely a stochastic process. But there are times when the market does setup with a probability scenario that provides you a foothold. Your job is to be consistent in trading those probability setups and trade them whenever they occur.

Trade sort of a cat. Most beginners over trade. It's one among the foremost common trading sins. Your job is to be better than other day traders in having the discipline to attend sort of a cat within the brush until just the proper moment (your high probability setup) then hop on the trade without hesitation.

Successful trading is just a game of not making mistakes. Keep an inventory of your day trading rules posted on the wall or on your monitor then follow those rules perfectly. you want to be more disciplined than the typical trader. Never depart from your rules regardless of how good a trade "looks" or "feels" to you if it violates your objective and back-tested rules.

Only trade once you are in an optimal spirit. Never trade once you are tired or are in an emotionally unstable situation (after a fight with a spouse or friend for example). Day trading is more like athletics than academics. Trading on such a brief time-frame requires you to be ready to make blink of eye decisions, and you're risking tons of cash once you do. confirm your mind is sharp and your emotions are centered.

Keep an in-depth trading log. a day trading course I've seen features a trading log. Yet my experience in handling trading students demonstrates that but 10% of them actually use it. this is often an enormous mistake. Not only do you have to log every trade, but you ought to also record how you felt and what you were thinking as you took the trade. during this way, your logs will become a kind of "biofeedback" mechanism for you. Personally, this was the difference that made all the difference on my behalf.

These 5-day trading rules aren't the sort of rules that you simply were probably trying to find. The masses want rules about indicators, price bars, where you get in, and where you get out.

Granted, you actually need clear objective rules about those things also. Yet thousands of traders have those sorts of rules, and yet still fail because those rules are about market action.

They fail because they do not have, or don't follow, the more important rules the principles about their own action.

If you discover yourself resisting the importance of those rules about your own behavior, realize that you simply are one among the masses who feels an equivalent way. But since the masses fail at day trading, you want to set yourself apart and do something different than them.

Online Trading - Day Trading Rules

So you're performing online trading and trade stocks and/or options and call yourself each day trader. does one know the wants of day trading? In our user's group, repeatedly this question comes up, and what happens if I accidentally (or on purpose) violate one among these rules? There are several variations of actions that will occur which will trigger day trading and that I will attempt to answer most of them. As each situation is different, I will be able to list the foremost common.

What Is Day Trading?

In this article, we are only discussing day trading because it pertains to stocks and options. Commodities and Forex don't have an equivalent day trading rules. I don't realize other trading disciplines.

If you purchase and sell a stock or option on an equivalent day, that's day trading. as an example, if you purchase 1000 shares of stock ABC (fictitious symbol) at 9:30 am and sell the 1000 shares of stock at 12:15 pm, you've got just entered into each day trade.

What Is a Pattern Day Trader?

A pattern day trader is defined in Exchange Rule 431 (Margin Requirement) as any customer who executes 4 or more same-day trades within any 5 successive business days and your day trading activities are greater than 6 percent of your total trading activity for that very same 5 day period (from FINRA web site).

What Are The Rules?

1. Account over $25k. -- To trade and not encounter any problems the equity in your trading account must be maintained over $25,000.

2. Buying/Selling the same day -- For accounts under $25k, if you purchase and sell an equivalent stock within the same day, any proceeds from that stock's sale can't be utilized in another trade thereon the same day. (May depend upon account.

My brokerage allows it but warns you about it.))

3. 3 times during a week -- you're allowed only 3 trades within 1 week (5 trading days). The 4th-day trade may subject you to a 90-day suspension of all day trading activities.

1. you'll get a 90-day suspension of all day trading activities.

2. Your account is often suspended for 90 days and no trading is going to be allowed therein account.

How to Avoid Problems?

1. Maintain a minimum of $25,000 equity in your trading account.

2. For accounts under $25,000 don't buy and sell an edge within the same day, hold your position overnight.

3. If you purchase and sell an equivalent stock/option within the same day, don't enter into a replacement trade where the monies from the sale of the stock just sold are going to be utilized in the acquisition of the new position.

4. If you've got purchased an edge from monies from a previous same-day sell, it's best to carry that position overnight.

5. don't perform each day trade activity quite 3 times every week .

MALINA PRONTO

Printed in Great Britain
by Amazon